Praying the Eucharist

 Prayers for personal use

Richard Harries

Illustrated by
Sr Ann Huston SSM

SPCK

For Luke, Toby and Ben

First published in Great Britain in 2004 by
Society for Promoting Christian Knowledge
Holy Trinity Church
Marylebone Road
London NW1 4DU

British Library Cataloguing-in-Publication Data
A catalogue record for this book is available from the
British Library

ISBN 0–281–05635–8

10 9 8 7 6 5 4 3 2 1

Designed and typeset by Kenneth Burnley, Wirral, Cheshire
Printed in Great Britain by Bookmarque

Contents

Front Piece

For the tradition which I handed on to you came to me from the Lord himself: that on the night of his arrest the Lord Jesus took bread, and after giving thanks to God broke it and said: 'This is my body, which is for you; do this in memory of me.' In the same way, he took the cup after supper, and said: 'This cup is the new covenant sealed by my blood. Whenever you drink it, do this in memory of me.' For every time you eat this bread and drink the cup, you proclaim the death of the Lord, until he comes.

1 Corinthians 11.23–26

Introduction

The Eucharist is an act of corporate worship. It is prayer that we engage in together. Therefore, the aim should be to attend to, to concentrate on, the actual words of the service, words which unite everyone present. So what is the justification of these 'Prayers for personal use'?

First, there are many spaces before, during and after a service where personal prayer is appropriate, where it is entirely proper to think one's own thoughts. These prayers and reflections are offered as a help for those personal thoughts and prayers at such times. Second, if the words of the services are truly to take us out of ourselves and lift us up to God, then we need to bring our self into the service and allow that self, with all our feelings and thoughts, to interact with the formal, corporate words of the service itself. It is all too easy for those words to remain dry and formal, detached from where we are and what we are feeling or thinking. Those words need to be filled out by who we are and what we bring to the service, in order that the person we are in reality might indeed be lifted up to God by the words of the liturgy.

Third, the structure and the words of the service itself need to be explicated and made our own. There are helpful books which seek to do this. This little book does not seek to replicate what others have done. Nevertheless, it does seek to provide in a handy, devotional form something of the meaning of the Eucharist.

So this is a book of personal prayers which is offered for use before, during and after a eucharistic gathering with the hope that it might illuminate and enrich our personal presence and participation.

A grey vertical line beside a prayer signals that the prayer may be said slowly, meditatively, with plenty of silence between each line. The prayers which are offered are not meant to be rigidly followed but rather to provide models for the kind of personal prayer we might want to offer at that point. Except where a few traditional prayers have been used, I have striven for a style which is simple, direct and accessible. Unless otherwise acknowledged in the text, the prayers have been written by me. Some of them were earlier published in *Praying Round the Clock*.[1] My hope is that this little book might prove of some help both to lifetime communicants and those just confirmed or recently admitted to communion.

Richard Harries
Oxford

The Night Before

As the watchman looks for the morning,
Even so our eyes wait for you, O Christ.
Come with the dawning of the day
And make yourself known to us in the breaking of
    bread;
For you are the risen Lord for ever and ever.

Traditional – sometimes used after compline

Before the Eucharist

When we arrive at church some of us seek silence, others seem to prefer to talk. Indeed the hubbub in some churches before a service begins makes it difficult for those who wish to be quiet. So I like the notice which some clergy put up in their churches:

Before the service, speak to God.
During the service, let God speak to you.
After the service, speak to one another.

*   *   *

Be still, my body.
Be still, my mind.
Be still, my soul.
Truly my soul waits still upon you, O God.
In your stillness you hold me still.

*   *   *

All we need, good Lord, is you yourself;
Not words about you, but your very presence.
In the silence,
In the stillness,
Come, Lord, come.

*   *   *

Who comes? To whom does he come? For what purpose does he come?

Reginald Somerset Ward[2]

O Christ, tirelessly you seek out those who are looking for you and who think that you are far away: teach us, at every moment, to place our spirit in your hands. While we are looking for you, already you have found us. No matter how poor our prayer is, you listen to us far beyond what we can imagine and believe.

Brother Roger of Taizé[3]

*   *   *

Set this down, then: Christianity is a meeting.

Lancelot Andrewes

*   *   *

Lord, you are present
As the fount from whom my being flows;
In the skill, care and beauty that have gone into this
    building,
In the prayers and devotion of those
Who have worshipped here over the years;
In the sacrament of the altar,
And in the heart of those about me;
Help me to be fully before you
As you are fully for us and with us.

*   *   *

Good Jesus,
I bring before you these past days.
For the good experiences, especially . . .
For all that nourished me and made me alive,
I give you thanks.
For all that I remember with unease, especially . . .
I hold in your healing presence.
For what is heavy on my heart and worrying away in
   my mind, especially . . .
I put in your upholding hands.

The Gathering

Collective prayer, then, is neither Jesus' prayer alone nor our prayer alone. It is a communion of prayer arising out of what the Anglican divine Richard Hooker called the 'Marvellous conjunction' between Christ the head of the church and us his body. His prayer is our prayer, and our prayer is his. In collective prayer we enact the exaltation made by the writer of the letter to the Hebrews when he beckons his readers to 'Draw near with a true heart in full assurance of faith' to the throne of the living God.

Charles Miller[4]

*   *   *

The president of the Eucharist may begin by saying the words 'In the name of the Father, and of the Son, and of the Holy Spirit'. To which we reply 'Amen'.

Our worship is Trinitarian and several times in the service this is brought home to us. The absolution and the blessing will use these words, for example. It is crucial to realize that this is not just a formula to safeguard Christian orthodoxy or a mere form of words. This is the very lifeblood of the Church and ourselves as Christians. We have Trinitarian words at the beginning of the service because the whole Eucharist is directed to the Father and this is only possible in the power of the Holy Spirit which comes to us through our union with Christ Jesus.

O God, Father,
Moment by moment you hold me in being,
On you I depend.

O God, eternal Son,
Friend and brother beside me,
In you I trust.

O God, Holy Spirit,
Life and love within me,
From you I live.

*   *   *

O God, you are from everlasting to everlasting
And all time is before you.
This moment, every moment, opens out
Into your eternity.
O God you are the boundless one,
In whom all bounds are enclosed.
This space, every space, stretches out
Into your endless spaciousness.
O God, you are the ever present one.
Be present now,
Today,
Always.

*   *   *

O God, Father,
Holding me in being,
O God, eternal Son,
Enfolding me with your love,
O God, Holy Spirit,
Filling me with your life.
God beyond me, God beside me, God within me,
Father, Son and Holy Spirit,
Ever to be worshipped and adored.

The liturgy has been to me a great theology teacher; a perpetual testimony that the Father, the Son and the Spirit, the one God blessed forever, is the author of all life, freedom, unity to men; that our prayers are nothing but responses to his voice speaking to us and in us.

F. D. Maurice

The Greeting

The president's initial task is to greet the people. There are few bolder statements with which to open an assembly than 'The Lord be with you', or 'Grace, mercy and peace from God our Father and the Lord Jesus Christ be with you' or the Easter greeting, 'Alleluia. Christ is risen.' These greetings need no supplementaries. For that reason, and for that reason alone, secular greetings such as 'Good morning' only serve to dumb down the eucharist, as if the president were a compère at some sort of chat show, patronising the rest of the community.

Kenneth Stevenson[5]

In the beginning,
Before time, before people,
Before the world began
GOD WAS

Here and now,
Among us, beside us,
Enlisting the people of earth
For the purposes of heaven
GOD IS

In the future,
When we have turned to dust
And all we know has found its fulfilment.
GOD WILL BE

Not denying the world but delighting in it,
Not condemning the world but redeeming it,
Through Jesus Christ
By the power of the Holy Spirit
GOD WAS, GOD IS,
GOD WILL BE.

The Iona Community[6]

Prayer of Preparation

Sweet Spirit,
Sweeten, cleanse and refresh
The springs of my being

*   *   *

O Spirit of God,
Who dost speak to spirits
Created in thine own likeness,
Penetrate into the depths of our spirits
Into the storehouse of memories,
Remembered and forgotten,
Into the depths of being
The very springs of personality.
And cleanse and forgive,
Making us whole and holy,
That we may be thine
And live in the new being
Of Christ our Lord.

Bishop George Appleton

*   *   *

Make me a clean heart, O God:
And renew a right spirit within me.

Psalm 51

I confess to you, holy and just God,
That I have sinned in thought, word and deed.
I have not loved you above all else,
Nor my neighbour as myself.
Through my sin I am guilty of more than I understand,
And share in the world's alienation from you.
Therefore I pray for help to see and break with my sins.
Forgive me for the sake of Jesus Christ.

Church of Sweden[7]

*   *   *

O God, give me honesty to recognize
That in the virtue on which I so pride myself
There is some seed of evil;
Gentleness to accept that in the dark rages and longings
    which so disturb me
There is some soul of good.
And grant me to strive after that integrity
Of deed and motive
Which you have revealed in Jesus.

Prayers of Penitence

O God, you have taught us that a broken
And contrite heart you will not despise.
Grant me the grace to be contrite.

*   *   *

From the cowardice that dare not face new truth
From the laziness which is contented with half truth
From the arrogance that thinks it knows all truth,
Good Lord, deliver me.

Prayer from Kenya

*   *   *

O Holy Spirit of God,
Help me to know myself
Without illusion or deception
And to know your mercy
Which never lets me go.

*   *   *

From all evil and mischief;
From pride, vanity and hypocrisy;
From envy, hatred and malice;
And from all evil intent,
Good Lord, deliver us.

From sloth, worldliness, and love of money;
From hardness of heart
And contempt for your word and your laws:
Good Lord, deliver us.

From sins of body and mind;
From the deceits of the world, the flesh, and the devil,
From error and false doctrine,
Good Lord, deliver us.

In all times of sorrow,
In all times of joy;
In the hour of death,
And at the day of judgement,
Good Lord, deliver us.

From the Alternative Service Book (ASB) litany

*   *   *

I am not worthy, master and Lord, that you should
come beneath the roof of my soul: yet, since you and
your love do wish to dwell in me, in boldness, I come.
You command, open the gates – which you alone have
forged; and you will come in with love toward all as is
your nature; you will come in and enlighten my
darkened reason. I believe that you will do this: for you
did not send away the harlot that came to you with
tears; nor cast out the repentant publican; nor reject the
thief who acknowledged your kingdom; nor forsake the
repentant persecutor, yet greater act; but all of those
who came to you in repentance, were counted in the
band of your friends, who alone abide blessed forever,
now and unto the endless ages.

St John Chrysostom

Grace strikes us when we are in great pain and
restlessness. It strikes us when we walk through the
dark valley of meaninglessness and empty life. It strikes
us when we feel that our separation is deeper than
usual, because we have violated another life, a life which
we loved, or from which we were estranged. It strikes us
when our disgust for our own being, our indifference,
our weakness, our hostility, and our lack of direction
and composure have become intolerable to us. It strikes
us when, year after year, the longed-for perfection of
life does not appear, when the old compulsions reign
with us as they have for decades, when despair destroys
all joy and courage. Sometimes at that moment a wave
of light breaks into our darkness, and it is as though a
voice were saying: 'You are accepted. *You are accepted!'*
accepted by that which is greater than you, and the
name of which you do not know. Do not ask for the
name now; perhaps you will find it later. Do not try to
do anything now; perhaps you will do much. Do not
seek for anything. *Simply accept the fact that you are
accepted.* If that happens to us, we experience grace.
After such an experience we may not be better than
before, and we may not believe more than before.
But everything is transformed. In that moment, grace
conquers sin, and reconciliation bridges the gulf of
estrangement. And nothing is demanded of this
experience, no religious or moral or intellectual
presupposition, nothing but *acceptance*.

Paul Tillich[8]

When the heart is hard and parched up,
Come upon me with a shower of mercy.
When grace is lost from life,
Come with a burst of song.
When tumultuous work raises its din on all sides,
Shutting me out from beyond,
Come to me, my Lord of silence,
With thy peace and rest.
When my beggarly heart sits crouched,
Shut up in a corner,
Break open the door, my king,
And come with the ceremony of a king.
When desire blinds the mind with delusion and dust,
O thou holy one, thou wakeful,
Come with thy light and thy thunder.

Rabindranath Tagore[9]

          *   *   *

Sinne is still hammering my heart
Unto a hardnesse, void of love:
Let suppling grace, to crosse his art,
                Drop from above.

George Herbert[10]

O Christ who holds the open gate,
O Christ who drives the furrow straight,
O Christ, the plough, O Christ the laughter
Of holy white birds flying after,
Lo, all my heart's field red and torn,
And thou wilt bring the young green corn,
The young green corn divinely springing,
The young green corn forever singing:
When the field is fresh and fair
Thy blessed feet shall glitter there.
And we will walk the weeded field,
And tell the golden harvests yield,
The corn that makes the holy bread,
By which the soul of man is fed,
The holy bread, the food unpriced,
Thy everlasting mercy, Christ.

John Masefield[11]

Gloria in Excelsis

The beauty of the world is Christ's tender smile for us coming through matter. He is really present in the universal beauty. The love of this beauty proceeds from God dwelling in our souls and goes out to God present in the universe.

Simone Weil[12]

We praise thee, O God, for thy glory
Displayed in all the creatures of the earth,
In the whale and the seal,
The starfish and the sturgeon,
The goat, the tiger, the rabbit and the stork;
The cedar and the jay.
They affirm thee in living,
All things affirm thee in living.

*   *   *

Late have I loved you, beauty so old and so new: late
have I loved you. And see, you were within and I was in
the external world and sought you there, and in my
unlovely state I plunged into those lovely created things
you made. You were with me and I was not with you . . .
You called and cried out loud and shattered my
deafness. You were radiant and resplendent, you put to
flight my blindness. You were fragrant and I drew in my
breath and now pant after you. I tasted you, and I feel
the hunger and thirst for you. You touched me, and I
am set on fire to attain the peace which is yours.

St Augustine[13]

*   *   *

We do not want merely to *see* beauty . . . we want
something else which can hardly be put into words . . .
to be united to the beauty we see, to pass into it, to
receive it into ourselves, to bathe in it, to become part
of it . . . At present we are on the outside of the world,
the wrong side of the door. We discern the freshness
and purity of the morning, but they do not make us
fresh and pure. We cannot mingle with the splendours

we see. But all the leaves of the New Testament are rustling with the rumour that it will not always be so. Some day, God willing, we shall get *in*. When human souls have become perfect in voluntary obedience as the inanimate creation is in its lifeless obedience, then they will put on its glory, or rather that greater glory of which nature is only the first sketch . . . We are summoned to pass through nature, beyond her, into that splendour which she fitfully reflects.

C. S. Lewis[14]

*   *   *

For she is the breath of the power of God,
And a pure emanation of the glory of the Almighty . . .
For she is more beautiful than the sun,
And excels every constellation of the stars . . .
She reaches mightily from one end of the earth to the
    other,
And she orders all things well.
I loved her and sought her from my youth,
And I desired to take her for my bride,
And I became enamoured of her beauty.

Wisdom of Solomon 7.25—8.2

*   *   *

For the God who said, 'Out of darkness light shall shine,' has caused his light to shine in our hearts, the light which is knowledge of the glory of God in the face of Jesus Christ.

2 Corinthians 4.6

The Collect

The collect is the Church's prayer for the week or a
particular day. It collects and focuses in a few short
phrases the prayers of God's people gathered together
here and throughout the world. We are part of a vast
company in earth and heaven. Prayer is like you and me
playing our second fiddles in an unending heavenly
symphony of praise and joy. When we pray we take up
our fiddles, and when we stop we put them down again
– but the music never stops.

Basil Moss

*   *   *

The prayers of the church are Christ's prayers,
particularly in the canon of the liturgy, where it is
entirely Christ praying . . . The characteristic of
Christian prayer is that it is the prayer of Christ,
brought to his father, from generation to generation in
constantly renewed situations, by those who, by grace
and participation, are Christ's presence in this world;
it is a continuous, unceasing prayer to God, that God's
will should be done, that all should happen according to
his wise and loving plan. This means that our life of
prayer is at the same time a struggle against all that is
not Christ's. We prepare the ground for our prayer each
time we shed something which is not Christ's, which is
unworthy of him, and only the prayer of one who can,
like St Paul, say 'I live, yet not I, but Christ liveth in
me' . . . is real Christian prayer.

Metropolitan Anthony of Sourozh[15]

The Liturgy of the Word

Readings

The situation of the reader of scripture is probably closest to that in which I read to others a letter from a friend . . . The distance between us would be clearly apparent as it was read. And yet I would also be unable to read the letter of my friend to others as if it were of no concern to me. I would read it with personal interest and regard. Proper reading of Scripture is not a technical exercise that can be learned; it is something

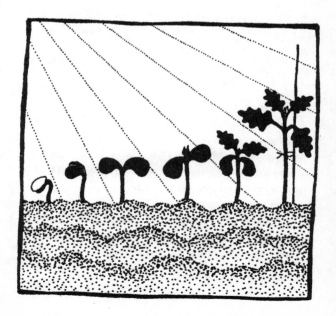

that grows or diminishes according to one's own
spiritual frame of mind.

Dietrich Bonhoeffer[16]

*   *   *

Attention to the word of God is an integral part of
every eucharistic celebration. This is not a matter of
mere liturgical rectitude. The reason why attention to
the word of God is integral to the eucharist is that it is
an essential element of Christian life. How do we listen
to the scriptures in the liturgy? Not as a collection of
individuals who happen to be in the same place at the
same time thinking any old thoughts that come into our
heads. It is as members of a community, as members of
the body of which Christ is the head, that we come
together to give our common attention to those words
and events which have brought us together and have
made us into this community . . . we come then to
attend and to give ourselves. The attention required of
us is in fact a kind of sacrifice.

Mark Santer[17]

*   *   *

O God, grant that hearing your word
We may understand and be touched by your glory;
Not with a short-lived enthusiasm
But with perseverance;
Not enticed by the false glamour and values of the world
But bringing forth the fruit of the Spirit in our lives,
    thirty fold, sixty fold, a hundred fold.

Based on the parable of the sower

Romano Guardini's words are worth quoting . . .

Solemn reading requires solemn listening, not simultaneous reading. Otherwise, why read aloud at all? Our bookish upbringing is to blame for this unnaturalness. Most deplorably, it encourages people to read when they should listen. As a result, the fairytale has died and poetry has lost its power: for its resonant, wise, fervent and festive language is meant to be heard.

The act of public reading is therefore the critical first element in the proclamation of the word. It is designed not chiefly to instruct or inform but to allure us into response to God's loving-kindness in prayer and praise.

For this hearing is meant to be the hearing of the heart. It is to be received into the depths of our being. The process of deep hearing begins as we actually hear the words spoken. That hearing, however, is but the beginning of a hearing which must reach deeply within us. If those words are to engage us at our spiritual centre something more is needed.

Charles Miller[18]

*   *   *

Both the reader and the listener play an equal part in enabling the word of God to be truly heard through the Scriptures. If the reader has carefully prepared the reading, so that they read it with understanding, and if they have practised reading it as though it were reading to others a letter from a friend, as Bonhoeffer suggested, then the listener, instead of immediately switching off, will be alerted to something of interest and importance. This attention of the listener will in turn make the reader, unconsciously, even more given over to the text before her. There is a mutually reinforcing cycle. A well-prepared reading arouses the attention of the listener and this in turn draws something from the reader. Too often, of course, it is the opposite cycle that is reinforced. An ill-prepared reading fails to arouse the attention of the congregation. The reader senses this and reads even more badly, which again leads the congregation to think of anything but the lesson.

Living Word,
Help me so to attend with my mind and hear with
    my heart
That all vain, wandering and self-preoccupied
    thoughts
May drop away;
Search, nourish and quicken me through these
    words
That my life may speak of the Father.

Sermon

God meets us in his word, in a concrete word, the
preaching instituted in Jesus Christ . . . The Word of
God is not a timeless statement, but a concrete word
addressed to men and women here and now.

Rudolf Bultmann

*   *   *

*Psalm 42.7 has the lovely words 'Deep calls unto deep'.
Cardinal Newman used them as the basis for his motto* 'Cor
ad cor loquitur', *heart speaks unto heart.*

May your Holy Spirit in her heart
Speak to your Holy Spirit in mine.

Gracious God, help us to love you above all else.
When we are weak, make us strong. When we are
discouraged, inspire us. When we are weary, renew us.
When we are faithless, bring us back to you, the source
of our hope, and the well of our deepest joy. Through
Jesus Christ our Lord.

Michael Townsend and Kenneth Stevenson[19]

*　　　*　　　*

Judge not the preacher; for he is thy judge:
If thou mislike him, thou conceiv'st him not.
God calleth preaching folly. Do not grudge
To pick out treasures from an earthen pot.
The worst speaks something good: if all wants sense,
God takes a text, and preacheth patience.

George Herbert[20]

*　　　*　　　*

O Thou eternal wisdom
Whom we partly know and partly do not know.
O Thou external justice, whom we partly acknowledge,
But never wholly obey.
O Thou eternal love, whom we love a little,
But fear to love too much.
Open our minds that we may understand,
Work in our wills that we may obey,
Kindle our hearts, that we may love,
Amen. Come, Lord Jesus.

T. R. Milford

The divine call, directed to each of us, seeks our response. As Gerard Hughes puts it, God is a 'Beckoning' word. Through his word proclaimed God beckons us toward a meeting, into conversation. His word is not to be lodged in the head as a bit of holy information but to descend to the heart, that deeper centre of ourselves. It is an approach to each of us in our absolute uniqueness. The contemporary Egyptian spiritual father Matta el Meskeen puts it this way when he speaks of our encounter with God through scripture: 'God speaks, and every human being on the face of the earth can hear this voice, understand and respond, as if he is being called personally by name.'

Charles Miller[21]

*   *   *

As I listen to these words
May I hear your Word:
A Word to understand and ponder
And act on.
A Word that brings me before you,
To know better what I am for,
And what I should do for you and for others.

The Creed

In one of the baptism services, after the candidates have made their declaration of faith the celebrant addresses the congregation as a whole in the words, 'This is the faith of the Church' and the congregation replies, 'This is our faith. We believe in God, Father, Son and Holy Spirit.' The creed is the faith of the Church, which is why in the most usual forms now we begin by saying 'We believe' rather than 'I believe'. This is in no way to take away from the crucial importance of our personal faith. But it is a recognition that before it is our faith it is the faith of the Church as a whole, and it is that faith which I have the privilege of sharing. This faith is not simply verbal assent to a number of propositions. It is fundamentally about trust, about putting our trust in God, whom Christians conceive in a particular way. At the same time, this does not mean that the statements of belief in the creed are unimportant. They quite rightly shape both our faith and our prayers. As Austin Farrer once wrote:

Prayer and dogma are inseparable. They alone can explain each other. Either without the other is meaningless and dead . . . Prayer is the active use or exercise of faith; and the creed defines the contours of that world on which faith trains her eyes . . . No dogma deserves its place unless it is prayable, and no Christian deserves his dogmas who does not pray them.[22]

*　　　*　　　*

Faith cannot be without an object. In the act of trust a man forsakes himself and anchors himself to a thing or person on which he relies. And consequently, since man cannot live without trust, he is dependent on the truly trustworthy becoming apparent to him. For Isaiah the God of Israel was truly trustworthy; and for the early Christians, who in the words of the Roman baptismal creed repeated their threefold 'I believe', it was the God whose son had appeared on earth in Jesus Christ and who is present through his spirit to those who believe in him. The eternal God, who revealed his love for men through Jesus Christ, was for them the unshakeable foundation on which a man can unconditionally build.

Wolfhart Pannenberg[23]

*   *   *

The first prayer below understands the creed primarily as an act of trust; the second stresses the importance of the way in which the Church articulates that trust.

(1)
> O God, ground of being,
> Upholding all things,
> On you I rest the weight of my life,
> Especially my worries at this time about . . .
> In you I trust:
> Not in my own puny faith
> But the faith of the Church,
> The faith of Christ himself,
> In his faith, for me and in me, I trust.

(2)

> O Holy Spirit, Spirit of truth
> Leading the Church into all truth
> We give you thanks for your illumination and
> guidance in the past,
> Which helped the Church articulate its faith in
> relation to the issues of those times.
> Lead us into the same truth
> As we seek to respond to the dilemmas which face
> us, especially . . .

*   *   *

I believe, although everything hides you from my faith.
I believe, although everything shouts No! to me …
I believe, although everything may seem to die.
I believe, although I no longer wish to live,
because I have founded my life
On a sincere word,
On the word of a friend,
On the word of God.

I believe, although I feel alone in pain.
I believe, although I see people hating.
I believe, although I see children weep,
because I have learnt with certainty
That he comes to meet us
In the hardest hours,
With his love and his light
I believe, but increase my faith.

From Livro de Cantos, *Porto Alegre, Brazil*[24]

The following words were written on a wall in a besieged Warsaw ghetto. In the midst of despair they express a profound Jewish hope. For Christians the hope is that this Messiah for which Jews long will be the revealing in glory of the humble, humiliated one.

I believe, I believe, I believe,
With a perfect faith
In the coming of the Messiah;
And in the coming of the Messiah I believe.
And even though he tarry
I nevertheless believe,
Even though he tarry
Yet, I believe in him.
I believe, I believe, I believe.

Prayers of Intercession

It is easy for the intercessions at the Eucharist to become formulaic and mechanical. It is good that they should have structure, as they do in Anglican services. It is also good that they should be carefully prepared. But structure and preparation pave the way for true prayer, they are not a substitute for it.

Very often the intercessions are introduced with the words:

In the power of the Spirit and in union with Christ Jesus let us pray to the Father.

This not only reminds us that Christian prayer is Trinitarian prayer, involving all members of the Holy Trinity, but that the Holy Spirit, in particular, has a key role to play. St Paul's words on the Spirit and prayer are fundamental.

In the same way the Spirit comes to the aid of our weakness. We do not even know how we ought to pray, but through our inarticulate groans the Spirit himself is pleading for us, and God who searches our inmost being knows what the Spirit means, because he pleads for God's people as God himself wills.

Romans 8.26–27

In the intercessions, as in the Eucharist as a whole, it is Christ praying in the Church, his body, to the Father. It is therefore right that we should bear in mind the whole sweep of his work, in the world and in the Church: and helpful to have an ordered way of remembering in prayer different parts of the Church and different aspects of the world.

But we can bring into this our own personal concerns. For one of the ways in which God works is through our prayers. Each one of us has a unique perspective on life and we bring to God what we see and no one else does. So although it is the intercession of the Church, it is filled out and focused by that unique contribution which each person brings to it, through their particular concern about something in the news or a particular part of the worldwide Church, in addition of course to more personal matters to do with people they know.

O Holy Spirit
Giver of light and life,
Impart to us thoughts higher than our own thoughts,
Prayers better than our own prayers,
Power beyond our own powers,
That we may spend and be spent
In the ways of love and goodness,
After the perfect image of our Lord and Saviour Jesus
    Christ.

Eric Milner-White[25]

The Church of Christ

O God of unchangeable power and eternal light, look favourably upon thy whole church, that wonderful and sacred mystery; and by the tranquil operation of thy perpetual providence carry out the work of our salvation; and let the whole world feel and see that the things which were cast down are being raised up; that those which had grown old are being made new; and that all things are returning into unity through him by whom all things were made, even Jesus Christ our Lord.

Gelasian Sacramentary[26]

*　　　*　　　*

Most gracious Father, we most humbly beseech thee for the holy Catholic Church. Fill it with all truth; in all truth with all peace. Where it is corrupt, purge it; where it is in error direct it; where anything is amiss, reform it; where it is right, strengthen and confirm it; where it is in want, furnish it; where it is divided and rent asunder, make up the breaches of it, O thou Holy One of Israel.

William Laud

Creation, Human Society, the Sovereign and Those in Authority

To clasp the hands in prayer is the beginning of an uprising against the disorder of the world.

Karl Barth

*　　　*　　　*

What would the world be, once bereft
Of wet and of wildness? Let them be left,
O let them be left, wildness and wet;
Long live the weeds and the wilderness yet.

Gerard Manley Hopkins[27]

Generations have trod, have trod, have trod;
And all is seared with trade; bleared, smeared with toil;
And wears man's smudge and shares man's smell; the
  soil
Is bare now, nor can foot feel, being shod.

And for all this, nature is never spent;
There lives the dearest freshness deep down things.

Gerard Manley Hopkins[28]

*　　　*　　　*

We beseech thee, O Lord our God, to set the peace of
heaven within the hearts of men, that it may bind the
nations also in a covenant which cannot be broken;
through Jesus Christ our Lord.

The Cuddesdon Office Book[29]

*　　　*　　　*

O God,
Who set before us the great hope
That your kingdom shall come on earth
And taught us to pray for its coming:
Give us grace to discern the signs of its dawning
And to work for the perfect day
When the whole world shall reflect your glory;
Through Jesus Christ our Lord.

Percy Dearmer

Uphold, O God, all those who experience hostility,
Harassment or persecution for their beliefs.
Be to them a light showing the way ahead;
A rock giving them strength to stand;
A song singing of all things overcome.

The Local Community

Thank you God for all those who have loved me,
    prayed for me and helped me on my way.
Bless my family and friends,
Those about me now
And those whom I will meet in this coming week.
May we be to each other a sign of your love.

Those Who Suffer

Here I am, Lord
Alone, in the long silence
Listening . . .
I hear, in the silence,
The cry of all the afflicted
The tiny moan of the unborn
The pain, the pity
The yearning aspirations of unnumbered hearts
And their joys.
Here they all are, Lord
I bring them to you.
Lift them in hands that labour, and that pray
Hands that are frail, and have no strength
But a burning desire to help
To heal, to comfort
To bring them all to you.

From within the Carmelite tradition

*　　　　*　　　　*

Almighty and everlasting God, the comfort of the sad,
the strength of them that suffer; let the prayers of thy
children who cry out of any tribulation come unto thee;
and unto thee every Christian soul that is distressed
grant thou mercy, grant relief, grant refreshment;
through Jesus Christ our Lord.

Gelasian and Liturgy of St Mark

'Daughters of Jerusalem, do not weep for me, but weep for yourselves and for your children.'

Luke 23.28

Jesus,
You have heard our tears:
The tears women have shed in silence
Because we were afraid to be heard;
The tears women have held back
Thinking we deserved violence;
The tears we have not held back
But were not comforted;
The tears women have wept alone
Because we would not ask to be held;

The tears women weep together
Because our sisters cannot feed their children;
Because our sisters live in fear;
Because the earth herself is threatened.

So we weep.

Christian Aid[30]

*   *   *   **

We hold in your presence, O God, all those who
    mourn.
Unlock their hearts that they may grieve,
Open their minds that they may find a new direction in
    their lives,
And grant them the comfort of your presence.

          *   *   *

O God, bless those who are careworn and burdened,
Grant them to know your care-free delight;
For from you all things spring forth,
Unto you all things run for refreshment.

          *   *   *

Most loving Lord,
When our hearts are wintry,
Grieving, or in pain
Thy touch can call us back to life again.
Fields of our hearts
That dead and bare have been:
Love is come again, like wheat
That springeth green.

From an Easter carol

The Communion of Saints

For all the saints
Who went before us
Who have spoken to our hearts
And touched us with your fire,
We praise you, O God.

For all the saints
Who live beside us
Whose weaknesses and strengths
Are woven into our own,
We praise you, O God.

For all the saints
Who live beyond us
Who challenge us
To change the world with them,
We praise you, O God.

Christian Aid[31]

The Liturgy of the Sacrament

The Peace

When the kiss of peace first started to be introduced into liturgies in the Church of England it is said that one person, when offered the peace, replied, 'No thank you, I'm Church of England.' The playwright Alan Bennett describes attending the requiem of an old lady who for fifteen years lived in a van in his garden and his own feeling as what he describes as 'The affirmation of fellowship' neared:

The old man, who was my neighbour, turned round and shook hands and with such an unselfconscious goodness that I was straight away put to shame and saw how in these circumstances my liturgical fastidiousness was sheer snobbery.

Alan Bennett[32]

*　　　*　　　*

Do not think that *this* kiss ranks with those given in public by common friends. It is not of that sort. *This* kiss blends souls with one another, and solicits for them entire forgiveness. Therefore the kiss is the sign that our souls are mingled together, and have banished all remembrance of wrongs. For this cause Christ said 'If you bring your gift . . . first be reconciled with your brother, and then come and offer your gift' . . . The kiss therefore is reconciliation and for this reason holy.

Cyril of Jerusalem[33]

Risen Christ
As you brought peace to the disciples in a locked
    room
So you bring peace to us now
As we greet one another in your name.
Penetrate the locked doors of our hearts,
Our suspicions, self-preoccupation and indifference
And permeate this place with your presence.

*   *   *

It will take some sawing
To be roundtabled.
Some redefining
And redesigning,
Some redoing and rebirthing
Of narrow long churching
Can painful be
For people and tables.
It would mean no daising
And throning,
For but one king is there
And he is a foot washer,
At table no less.

The bottom narrow long ministers
When they confront
A roundtable people,
After years of working up the table
To finally sit at its head,
Only to discover that the table has been turned round?

It must be loved into roundness,
For God has called of people
Not 'Them and us'.
'Them and us' are unable
To gather round;
For at a roundtable
There are no sides
And ALL are invited
To wholeness and to food.

Roundtabling means
No preferred seating,
No first and last,
No better, and no corners
For the 'Least of these'.
Roundtabling means
Being with,
A part of,
Together and one.
It means room for the spirit
And gifts
Disturbing profound peace for all.

Chuck Lathrop[34]

Your peace, O Christ, unites heaven and earth
And holds us here with you.
'God's people come in all shapes and sizes.'
We have different backgrounds and interests, likes
and dislikes
Yet all are one in you.
Take us with all our foibles and frailty, our meanness
and kindness
That we may give and receive from one another
The peace you have promised, which the world
cannot give.

*   *   *

O God:
Enlarge my heart
That it may be big enough to receive the greatness of
your love.
Stretch my heart
That it may take into it all those who with me around
the world
Believe in Jesus Christ.
Stretch it
That it may take into it all those who do not know him,
But who are my responsibility because I know him
And stretch it
That it may take in all those who are not lovely in my
eyes:
And whose hands I do not want to touch;
Through Jesus Christ, my saviour.

Prayer of an African Christian[35]

Preparation of the Table

If you wish to understand what is meant by 'The Body of Christ', listen to the apostle saying to the faithful, 'You are the Body of Christ and his member' (1 Cor. 12.27). It is the mystery of yourselves that is laid on the table; it is the mystery of yourselves that you receive. To that which you answer 'Amen', and in answering you assent. For you hear the words 'The Body of Christ', and you reply 'Amen'. Be a member of the Body of Christ, that the *Amen* may be true. If you have received well, you *are* that which you have received.

There you are on the table, there you are in the chalice.

St Augustine[36]

*　　　*　　　*

Jesus, I receive your love
Poured out for me
In bread and wine.
Accept this gift of my life,
Brought to the altar
Without conditions.
Do your work in me
And let me be, like you,
Taken, blessed,
And given for others,
For, in spite of my sin,
You know that I love you.

Angela Ashwin[37]

As this bread was once scattered seed, O Lord of life,
Sown in the earth to die and rise to new life,
So gather all peoples together
In the one humanity that is your purpose for us.
Restore the broken life of your creation,
Heal the disfigured body of your world,
And draw us all into yourself
Through your cross and in the power of your risen life.

Worship in an Indian context[38]

*   *   *

God of all places and this place:
You promised a new earth
Where the hungry will feast
And the oppressed go free.
Come Lord, build that place among us.

God of all times and this time:
You promised a new day
When the fearful will laugh
And the sick find healing.
Come Lord, speed that time among us.

God of all people, our God:
Take what we have and what we hope for
Make this a world where the poor find good news.
We come Lord, to share in the work of your kingdom
Until the new earth is created among us.

Christian Aid[39]

Taking of the Bread and Wine

He prays for us, as our priest; he prays in us as our
head; he is prayed to by us, as our God. Let us
recognize then our words in him, and his words in us.

St Augustine

*   *   *

Warmly you welcome me, O gracious God,
At the great feast.
Moment by moment you invite me
To share with others in the delight of your world.
Now, you feed me with your own divine life
That all may be utterly changed.
Change me
Change your Church.
Transform your world, so that all in need,
The hungry, the lonely, the suffering, the spiritually
    lost,
The oppressed, the brutalized, all
May find a place at the table of life
And so be made ready for that divine banquet
In which all things find their fulfilment and joy.

*   *   *

Lord, this is thy feast,
    prepared by thy longing,
    spread at thy command,
    attended at thine invitation,
    blessed by thine own word,
    distributed by thine own hand,
    the undying memorial of thy sacrifice upon the cross,
    the full gift of thine everlasting love,
    and its perpetuation till time shall end.

Lord, this is Bread of heaven, Bread of life,
    that, who so eateth, never shall hunger more
    and this the cup of pardon, healing, gladness, strength,
    that whoso drinketh, thirsteth, not again
So may we come, O Lord, to thy table;
Lord Jesus, come to us.

Eric Milner-White[40]

*   *   *

O Lord, I want to love you,
To love you above all things;
For you are my supreme good,
And the source of all that is good.
So grant, on top of all your other gifts,
The heart to love,
A heart full of love for you;
A true love,
Not a fancy or a feeling,
But real, tough, persevering.

O God, you promise a world
Where those who now weep shall laugh;
   Those who are hungry shall feast;
   Those who are poor now,
   And excluded,
   Shall have your kingdom for their own.
I want this world too.
I renounce despair.
I will act for change.
I choose to be included
in your great feast of life.

Christian Aid[41]

The Eucharistic Prayer

But what of our own personal eucharistic prayers
offered as the climax of our response to God's word?
As far as we know the eucharistic prayer has never
included silence for such prayers as does collective
praying. So how is our private prayer integrated into
the collective prayer of the great thanksgiving? Clearly
a different and more subtle integration is called for.
Instead of employing a designated silent space at the
offering for private eucharistic prayer, the integration of
the private and the corporate must be achieved, I think,
by a thanksgiving-orientated spirituality. Such a
spirituality, rooted in St Paul's vision of Christian life as
perpetual thanksgiving, needs to become the overall
context or spiritual disposition in which the great
thanksgiving is heard and prayed. That eucharistic
prayer then becomes the centrepiece from a
tremendously wide chorus of thanksgiving to which
every member of the congregation contributes.

Charles Miller[42]

*   *   *

The word 'Eucharist' comes from the Greek for thanksgiving.
Poets down the ages have drawn us into their appreciation of
different aspects of life. Rupert Brooke, for example, began a
poem:

These I have loved:
White plates and cups, clean-gleaming.[43]

He then went on for another 31 lines listing all the things he loved. Elizabeth Jennings began a poem, 'I count the moments of my mercies up' and continued:

Others examine consciences. I tell
My beads of gracious moments shining still.
I count my good hours and they guide me well.[44]

So we bring into this Eucharist all the different aspects of life, sometimes quirky, sometimes fun, from our own unique perspective, that we love. It might be a list even longer than Rupert Brooke's 31 lines. Like Elizabeth Jennings we can count the gracious moments in our lives and the good hours.

At the heart of our thanksgiving, however, is the life, death and the resurrection of Jesus. W. H. Auden wrote a poem in which he said he could find reasons enough to face the sky and roar in anger and despair. Most of us will have felt like that at one time or another. Auden then went on to say that if we roar at the sky it would only reiterate:

That singular command
I do not understand
'Bless what there is for being'.[45]

We are able, despite everything, to 'Bless what there is for being' because, in Jesus, God shares our life to the full, with all its anguish and sense of God-forsakenness. In all our pain and puzzlement God is with us and for us. So in the Eucharist our thanks comes to a focus in Jesus. In him all our personal thanksgiving is undergirded and grounded. And here once again Jesus gives himself to us and feeds us with his own divine life.

Blessed art Thou, O Lord our God, King of the universe,
For the mystery and marvel of being alive.
Blessed art Thou, O Lord our God, King of the universe
Who has created us in a world
Which arouses and delights the senses.

*   *   *

Thank you, Lord, for all that is good;
Satisfying work and innocent pleasure,
Contentment and affection
For all that is fulfilling,
For all that warms us through,
For all that is strong and healthy,
We bless your holy name, O Lord.

*   *   *

Thank you God
For all who support us with their love and prayers,
For all kindliness and generosity,
For all who, in misfortune and adversity,
Have become more transparent to your light within
    them,
Revealing your love.

*   *   *

For some people the eucharistic prayers that we have in our present authorized prayer books do not draw enough on the feminine imagery of the Bible. So here is one which does:

Eternal wisdom, source of our being,
And goal of all our longing,
We praise you and give you thanks
Because you have created us, women and men,
Together in your image
To cherish your world and seek your face.
Divided and disfigured by sin,
While we were yet helpless,
You emptied yourself of power,
And took upon our unprotected flesh.
You laboured with us upon the cross,
And have brought us forth
To the hope of resurrection.

Therefore, with the woman who gave you birth,
The women who befriended you and fed you,
Who argued with you and touched you,
The woman who anointed you for death,
The women who met you, risen from the dead,
And with all your lovers throughout the ages,
We praise you saying:

Holy, holy, holy
Vulnerable God, heaven and earth are full of your
**   glory;**
Hosanna in the highest.

**Blessed is the one
Who comes in the name of God;
Hosanna in the highest.**

       *   *   *

Blessed is our brother Jesus,
Who, before his suffering, earnestly desired
To eat with his companions
The Passover of liberation;
Who on the night that he was betrayed,
Took bread, gave thanks, broke it and said:
'This is my body, which is for you.
Do this to remember me.'

In the same way also the cup, after supper,
Saying: 'This cup is the new covenant in my blood.
Do this, whenever you drink it,
To remember me.'

Christ has died
Christ is risen
Christ will come again.

Therefore, as we eat this bread and drink this cup,
We are proclaiming Christ's death until he comes.
In the body broken and the blood poured out,
We restore to memory and hope
The broken and unremembered victims
Of tyranny and sin;
And we long for the bread of tomorrow
And the wine of the life to come.
Come then, life-giving spirit of our God,
Brood over these bodily things,
And make us one body with Christ;
That we may labour with creation
To be delivered from its bondage to decay
Into the glorious liberty
Of all the children of God.

Janet Morley[46]

*   *   *

Prayer is a state of continual gratitude.

St John of Kronstadt

The Lord's Prayer

The Our Father contains all possible petitions . . . it is impossible to say it once through, giving the fullest possible attention to every word without a change, infinitesimal perhaps but real, taking place in the soul.

Simone Weil[47]

*   *   *

The fact that Christ and we become one, means that what applies to Christ applies to us, and that we can, in a way unknown to the rest of the world, call God our Father, no longer by analogy, no longer in terms of anticipation or prophecy, but in terms of Christ. This has a direct bearing upon the Lord's Prayer: on the one hand, the prayer can be used by anyone, because it is universal, it is the ladder of our ascent towards God, on the other hand, it is absolutely particular and exclusive: it is the prayer of those who are, in Christ, the sons of the eternal Father, who can speak to him as sons.

Metropolitan Anthony of Sourozh[48]

*   *   *

When I am down and helpless
When lies are raining
When fear and indifference are growing
May your kingdom come.

When joy is missing
When love is missing
And unbelief is growing
May your kingdom come.

To the sick and lonely
To the imprisoned and tortured
May your kingdom come.

Into the churches
Into our praying, into our singing
May your kingdom come.

Into our hearts
Into our hands, into our eyes
May your kingdom come. Soon!

Czech litany[49]

*   *   *

'Our daily bread' is one of the possible ways of
translating the Greek text. This bread, which in Greek
is called *epiousion* may be daily, but it may also be the
bread that is beyond substance. The Fathers of the
Church, beginning with Origen and Tertullian, have
always interpreted this passage as referring not only to
our human needs but also to the mysterious bread of
the eucharist. Unless we are fed in this new way,
mysteriously, by divine bread (because we depend now
for our existence on God alone) we will not survive
(John 6.53). God sent to his people the manna and gave
them water from the rock, struck by the rod of Moses.
The two gifts are images of Christ: 'Man shall not live
by bread alone but by every word that proceedeth from
the mouth of God.' This is what Christ recalled from
the Old Testament (Deut. 8.3) to confound Satan. This
'word' is not simply words but first of all the Word that
resounds for ever, upholding all things created, and

then also the Word incarnate, Jesus of Nazareth; furthermore, it is the bread of which manna was the image, the bread which we receive in communion. The waters that ran and filled the brooks and the rivers at the command of Moses, are the image of that water which was promised to the Samaritan woman and of the blood of Christ which is our life.

Metropolitan Anthony of Sourozh[50]

*   *   *

To have something to forgive represents quite a programme. In any reflecting on hurt, somewhere near the beginning one needs to ask what exactly can be done about it. The conventional hope is in the external solution, in some change in the offender altering everything for the better, with the resentment dispelled by the offender's acknowledgement, regret, apology and resolve not to offend again. Sometimes this happens, but not always; and sometimes it happens to such little effect in the wounded heart that it is a question what exactly it amounts to, since it is clear that something else has to happen to bring release there.

It is the release in the wounded heart that matters. When that release comes it often so changes the sufferer's attitude to the offender that his acknowledgement and apology become secondary affairs, whether they have or have not yet occurred.

That is the true release, because it is the point of growth in the whole situation. The true release is not when a state of tension and grievance is brought to an end. It is when the conflict situation is transformed into one of new possibility so that it becomes a new beginning.

Time spent in thinking about the inwardness of forgiveness is one of the better ways of spending time. Forgiveness is a programme of work you have to do on yourself. It is a blessing that, primarily at any rate, does not reside in any change in the other person, in some contrite act on his part.

J. Neville Ward[51]

*   *   *

There is something poignant in the last two-fold petition of the Lord's Prayer, 'Lead us not into temptation, but deliver us from evil'. It is a simple cry for help where it is needed most. There is something stripped and urgent about it. If we are wise, too, we shall see that it does not only need to be prayed when we are aware of the big test of fate that may lie ahead. It needs to be prayed in far more normal circumstance. 'Sometimes', says Bonhoeffer penetratingly, 'The attack of temptation takes the form of a false sense of security.' Our betrayal of Christ may not take place when we are being severely tested in the most obvious way, by grief and suffering, but when we are letting our souls take their ease.

The cry has about it the human honesty that we ought to show in prayer. It is a form of the cry of the father who brought his epileptic son to Jesus, and was asked whether he believed. 'I have faith, help me when faith falls short.' There is nothing more human in the whole of this prayer. Jesus knew that he was giving a prayer to us ordinary human beings.

Kenneth Slack[52]

Breaking of the Bread

Lord Jesus Christ,
Because you broke bread with the poor,
You were looked on with contempt.

Because you broke bread with the sinful and outcast,
You were looked on as ungodly.

Because you broke bread with the joyful,
You were called a wine bibber and a glutton.
Because you broke bread in the upstairs room,
You sealed your acceptance of the way of the cross.

Because you broke bread on the way to Emmaus,
You made scales fall from the disciples' eyes.

Because you broke bread and shared it,
We will do so too, and ask your blessing.

Quoted by Janet Morley[53]

*   *   *

*John the Baptist referred to Jesus as 'The Lamb of God'
(John 1.36). This image, drawn from the Old Testament
sacrificial system, is used in the New Testament to bring out
the willingness of Jesus to suffer 'For the sin of the whole
world', as the eucharistic prayer in the Book of Common
Prayer puts it. This is the theme of the Agnus Dei which has
been part of the liturgy since the seventh century. The world
'mercy' in Greek means much more than asking someone with
power over us not to use it. It means compassion and pity. We
look to 'some infinitely gentle suffering thing' to take away
the sin of the world.*

Daily, O God, we are lacerated by the evil of the world,
The hatred that leads to shooting and bombing and the
loss of innocent life,
The callousness that pushes aside those who don't
count,
The ruthless pursuit of self-interest, personal, national
and economic, at the expense of others,
The lack of respect for the earth, for the bodies of
others, for ourselves,
The indifference that leaves those who suffer to go on
suffering,
All this goes on hammering in the nails in your hands
on the cross.
Have pity on your benighted world
Take away our sin
Take away our terrible sin
And grant us the peace of reconciliation with one
another and you.

Giving of Communion

'Twas God the Word that spake it,
He took the bread and brake it;
And what the Word did make it
That I believe it and take it.

Attributed to Queen Elizabeth I

*   *   *

Ernest Raymond was a priest who, after World War I, wrote a best-selling novel. He lost his faith but towards the end of his life came back to belief. This is reflected in his novel The Bethany Road:

Now it was the Communion of the Faithful, and as I watched the people going up to the altar rails I was still only thinking dreamily. My mind wandered away to many other things than the wish that I could, once again, go up with them . . . Then all of a sudden, I was aware of a steady direction in my thoughts. It was as if I were being impelled along this straight path from behind or perhaps drawn along it from in front because there was a light in the distance . . . 'Surely, I decided, the only thing to do is to give oneself to a love one feels, and leave all else with the God unknown.' Next time then – perhaps one day – I would go up with the people and share with them in their communion. I would go in a kind of blind love and trust, asking pardon all the way for any unworthiness in a faith so unsure . . . Am I then home again at last? I do not know. Perhaps I shall never know. I hope and trust and do not know.[54]

If any be a devout lover of God, let him partake with gladness from this fair and radiant feast.

If any be a faithful servant, let him enter rejoicing into the joy of his Lord.

If any have wearied himself with fasting, let him now enjoy his reward.

If any have laboured from the first hour, let him receive today his rightful due.

If any have come after the third, let him celebrate the feast with thankfulness.

If any have arrived after the sixth, let him not be in doubt, for he will suffer no loss.

If any have delayed until the ninth, let him not hesitate but draw near.

If any have arrived only at the eleventh, let him not be afraid because he comes so late.

For the master is generous and accepts the last even as the first. He gives rest to him who comes at the eleventh hour in the same way as him who has laboured from the first. He accepts the deed, and commends the intention.

Enter then, all of you, into the joy of our Lord. First and last, receive alike your reward. Rich and poor, dance together. You who have fasted and you who have not fasted, rejoice today. The table is fully laden: let all enjoy it. Let the calf be fatted: let none go away hungry.

Let none lament his poverty; for the universal kingdom is revealed. Let none bewail his transgressions; for the light of forgiveness has risen from the tomb. Let none fear death; for the death of the saviour has set us free.

Homily read at the Easter midnight service in the Orthodox Church, attributed to St John Chrysostom

Almighty and everlasting God, behold we approach the
     sacrament of thy only-begotten Son, our Lord Jesus
     Christ.
As sick, we come to the physician of life;
As unclean, to the fountain of mercy;
As blind, to the light of eternal splendour;
As needy, to the Lord of heaven and earth;
As naked, to the King of Glory.

St Thomas Aquinas

*   *   *

In the act of communion our home-coming is
accomplished. Not that we do it only once. The whole
of life is a pattern of going and returning, of straying
and coming home. Whereas we are prodigal, God our
Father is constant in his love and ever welcoming when
we respond to his call. Christians gather for the
eucharist not once but again and again as if to express
the father's perennial call to us to hope for our return.
Like the father in Jesus' parable our Heavenly Father is
always ready with the feast when we, his prodigal
children, come home. And every home-coming is
different, just as every embrace is. What remains the
same is the limitless loving-kindness of the father who
is alpha and omega, our beginning and our end.

Charles Miller[55]

Christ is present and active, in various ways, in the entire eucharistic celebration. It is the same Lord who through the proclaimed word invites his people to his table, who through his minister presides at that table, and who gives himself sacramentally in the Body and Blood of his paschal sacrifice. It is the Lord present at the right hand of the Father, and therefore transcending the sacramental order, who thus offers to his Church, in the eucharistic signs, the special gift of himself.

The sacramental Body and Blood of the saviour are present as an offering to the believer awaiting his welcome. When this offering is met by faith, a life-giving encounter results. Through faith Christ's presence – which does not depend on the individual's faith in order to be the Lord's real gift of himself to his church – becomes no longer just a presence *for* the believer, but also a presence *with* him. Thus, in considering the mystery of the eucharistic presence, we must recognise both the sacramental sign of Christ's presence and the personal relationship between Christ and the faithful which arises from that presence.

Anglican-Roman Catholic International Commission (ARCIC)

Prayer after Communion

When Jesus Christ leads us to the holy table and gives us his own body to eat, he transforms us completely and changes us into what he is himself. Marked now by the impress of the royal seal, our clay is clay no longer, but itself becomes the very body of the king . . .

Under normal circumstances food is changed into the person who consumes it: fish, bread and the like become human flesh and blood. But in Holy Communion the exact opposite happens. The bread of life himself changes the person who eats, assimilating and transforming him into himself.

See in what sense the kingdom of heaven is within us.

Nicolas Cabasilas[56]

*   *   *

God, food of the poor;
Christ our bread,
Give us a taste of the tender bread
From your creation's table;
Bread newly taken
From your heart's oven
Food that comforts and nourishes us.
A fraternal loaf that makes us human
Joined hand in hand,
Working and sharing.
A warm loaf that makes us a family;
Sacrament of your body,
Your wounded people.

Quoted by Janet Morley[57]

In the silence
In the stillness
We rest in your presence
With us
Within us
In this union with you
This holy communion.
All things come from you, O God,
And moment by moment you hold me in being.
Now you have fed and filled me
With your own divine life
Changing me
That I may be a sign of your presence in the world.

*   *   *

Almighty and everlasting God, we most heartily thank
thee, for that thou dost vouchsafe to feed us, who have
duly received these holy mysteries, with the spiritual food
of the most precious Body and Blood of thy Son our
Saviour Jesus Christ; and dost assure us thereby of thy

favour and goodness towards us; and that we are very members incorporate in the mystical body of thy Son, which is the blessed company of all faithful people; and are also heirs through hope of thy everlasting kingdom, by the merits of the most precious death and passion of thy dear Son. And we most humbly beseech thee, O heavenly Father, so to assist us with thy grace, that we may continue in that holy fellowship, and do all such good works as thou hast prepared for us to walk in; through Jesus Christ our Lord, to whom, with thee and the Holy Ghost, be all honour and glory, world without end.

Book of Common Prayer

*   *   *

For the darkness of waiting
Of not knowing what is to come
But staying ready and quiet and attentive,
We praise you O God:

**For the darkness and the light
Are both alike to you.**

For the darkness of staying silent
For the terror of having nothing to say
And for the greater terror
Of needing to say nothing,
We praise you O God:

**For the darkness and the light
Are both alike to you.**

For the darkness of loving
In which it is safe to surrender
To let go of our self-protection
And to stop holding back our desire,
We praise you O God:

For the darkness and the light
Are both alike to you.

For the darkness of choosing
When you give us the moment
To speak, and act, and change
And we cannot know what we have set in motion,
But we still have to take the risk,
We praise you O God:

For the darkness and the light
Are both alike to you.

For the darkness of hoping
In a world which longs for you,
For the wrestling and labouring of all creation
For wholeness and justice and freedom,
We praise you O God:

For the darkness and the light
Are both alike to you.

Janet Morley[58]

Lord,
You are the deepest wisdom,
The deepest truth,
The deepest love
Within me.
Lead me in your way.

The Dismissal

In each of our lives Jesus comes as the bread of life – to be eaten, to be consumed by us. This is how he loves us. Then Jesus comes in our human life as the hungry one, the other, hoping to be fed with the bread of our life, our hearts loving, and our hands serving.

Mother Teresa of Calcutta

Gracious God
For the gift of life
With all its struggle
And great opportunity
I give you thanks.

For Jesus the life-giver
In whom we have life with you,
Now and forever
I give you thanks.

For the Holy Spirit
Making us alive
With his life
I give you thanks.

Open me to that Spirit
And renew your Church,
That we may share your life
With others.

Draw them into your love
And transform your world.

*   *   *

This prayer was found in the handbag of a famous theatre director, Lilian Baylis, when she died.

O Holy Spirit of God –
Come into my heart and fill me:
I open the windows of my soul to let thee in.
I surrender my whole life to thee:
Come and possess me, fill me with light and truth.
I offer to thee the one thing I really possess,
My capacity for being filled by thee.
Of myself I am an unprofitable servant,
An empty vessel.
Fill me so that I may live the life of the Spirit:
The life of truth and goodness, the life of beauty and
      love,
The life of wisdom and strength.
And guide me today in all things:
Guide me to the people I should meet or help:
To the circumstances in which I can best serve thee,
Whether by my action, or by my sufferings.
But, above all, make Christ to be formed in me,
That I may dethrone self in my heart
And make him king.
Bind and cement me to Christ by all thy ways
Known and unknown:
By holy thoughts and unseen graces,
And sacramental ties:
So that he is in me, and I in him,
Today, and for ever.

W. J. Carey

Risen, ascended, glorified Lord,
Grant that I may be in such solidarity with those who
    lose out now
That I too may be one of the poor whom you
    pronounce blessed;
And grant that I may so stand against the forces that
    crush the powerless,
Looking and working for your new order of love,
Trusting in you,
That even now I may be filled with the richness of your
    presence
And know the glory of your kingdom.

*   *   *

May the blessing of light be on you,
Light without and light within.
May the blessed sunlight shine upon you
And warm your heart
Till it glows like a great fire
And strangers may warm themselves
As well as friends.

Let the light shine out of the eyes of you,
Like a candle set
In the window of a house,
Bidding the wanderer to come in
Out of the storm.

May the blessing of rain be on you;
The soft sweet rain.
May it fall upon your spirit
So that little flowers may spring up
And shed their sweetness on the air.

And may the blessing of the great rains be on you,
To beat upon your spirit
And wash it fair and clean;
And leave there many a shining pool
Where the blue of heaven shines,
And sometimes a star.

May the blessing of the earth be on you,
The great round earth.
May you ever have a kindly greeting for people
As you are going along the roads.

And now may the Lord bless you,
And bless you kindly, Amen.

Irish blessing[59]

*   *   *

God the Sender, send us,
God the Sent, come with us,
God the strengthener of those who go, empower us,
That we may go with you
And find those who call you
Father, Son and Holy Spirit.

The Church in Wales

End Piece

Was ever another command so obeyed? For century
after century, spreading slowly to every continent and
country and among every race on earth, this action has
been done, in every conceivable human circumstances,
for every conceivable human need from infancy and
before it to extreme old age and after it, from the
pinnacles of earthly greatness to the refuge of fugitives
in the caves and dens of the earth. Men have found no
better thing than this to do for kings at their crowning
and for criminals going to the scaffold; for armies in
triumph or for a bride and bridegroom in a little
country church; for the proclamation of a dogma or for
a good crop of wheat; for the wisdom of the Parliament
of a mighty nation or for a sick old woman afraid to die;
for a schoolboy sitting an examination or for Columbus
setting out to discover America; for the famine of whole
provinces or for the soul of a dead lover; in thankfulness
that my father did not die of pneumonia; for a village
headman much tempted to return to fetish because the
yams had failed; because the Turk was at the gates of
Vienna; for the repentance of Margaret; for the
settlement of a strike; for a son for a barren woman; for
Captain so-and-so, wounded and prisoner of war; while
the lions roared in the nearby amphitheatre; on the
beach at Dunkirk; while the hiss of the scythes in the
thick June grass came faintly through the windows of
the church; tremulously, by an old monk on the fiftieth
anniversary of his vows; furtively, by an exiled bishop

who had hewn timber one day in a prison camp near Murmansk; gorgeously, for the canonization of S Joan of Arc – one could fill many pages with the reasons why men have done this, and not tell a hundredth part of them. And best of all, week by week, month by month, on a hundred successive Sundays, faithfully, unfailingly, across all the parishes of Christendom, the pastors have done this just to *make* the *plebs sancta Dei* – the holy common people of God.

Dom Gregory Dix[60]

Notes

1 Richard Harries, *Praying Round the Clock*, Mowbray, 1983
2 Bishop E. R. Morgan, *Reginald Somerset Ward: His Life and Letters*, Mowbray, 1963, p. 83
3 Letter to the author
4 Charles Miller, *Praying the Eucharist*, SPCK, 1995, p. 28
5 Kenneth Stevenson, *Do This: The Shape, Style and Meaning of the Eucharist*, Canterbury Press, 2002, p. 88
6 The Iona Community – used at the Oxford Diocesan Convention in 2002
7 From their order of the Mass
8 Paul Tillich, *The Shaking of the Foundations*, SCM Press, 1957, pp. 161–2
9 Rabindranath Tagore, 'Gitanjali', *Collected Poems and Plays*, Macmillan, 1916
10 George Herbert, 'Grace', *Complete English Works*, ed. Ann Pasternak Slater, Everyman, 1995, p. 58
11 John Masefield, 'The everlasting mercy', *Collected Poems*, Heinemann, 1924, p. 129
12 Simone Weil, *Waiting on God*, Fontana, 1959, p. 120
13 St Augustine, *Confessions*, trns. Henry Chadwick, OUP, 1992, p. 201
14 C. S. Lewis, 'The Weight of Glory', *Screwtape Proposes a Toast*, Fontana, 1965, pp. 106f.
15 Anthony of Sourozh, *Living Prayer*, Darton, Longman and Todd, 1966, pp. 72, 79.
16 Dietrich Bonhoeffer, *Life Together*, SCM Press, 1954, p. 56
17 Mark Santer, *The Church's Sacrifice*, Sisters of the Love of God Press, 1975, p. 3 – quoted in Stevenson, *Do This*
18 Miller, *Praying the Eucharist*, p. 36
19 Letter to the author from Kenneth Stevenson
20 Herbert, 'The church-porch', *Complete English Works*, p. 21
21 Miller, *Praying the Eucharist*, p. 39
22 Austin Farrer, *Lord I Believe*, Faith Press, 1958, pp. 9–10

23 Wolfhart Pannenberg, *The Apostles' Creed in the Light of Today's Questions*, SCM Press, 1972, pp. 4–5 – quoted in Stevenson, *Do This*

24 Quoted by Janet Morley, *Bread of Tomorrow*, SPCK, 1992, p. 110

25 Eric Milner-White, *My God, My Glory*, SPCK, 1954, p. 56, slightly adapted

26 *Gelasian Sacramentary*. A sacramentary was one of the liturgical books in use down to the thirteenth century for the celebrant at Mass. This is from one of the sacramentaries associated with Pope Gelasius, who died in 496

27 Gerard Manley Hopkins, 'Inversnaid', *The Poems of Gerard Manley Hopkins*, ed. W. H. Gardner and N. H. Mackenzie, OUP, 1970, p. 89

28 Hopkins, 'God's grandeur', *Poems of Gerard Manley Hopkins*, p. 66

29 *The Cuddesdon Office Book*, Oxford University Press, 1940, p. 179

30 Christian Aid, quoted in Morley, *Bread of Tomorrow*, p. 100

31 Christian Aid, quoted in Morley, *Bread of Tomorrow*, p. 162

32 Alan Bennett, 'Comfortable Words', *Writing Home*, Faber, 1994, p. 356 – quoted in Stevenson, *Do This*

33 Cyril of Jerusalem, *Mystagogical Catecheses*, 5.3 – quoted in Stevenson, *Do This*

34 Chuck Lathrop, 'In search of a round table', *The Good Wine: Spiritual Renewal in the Church of England*, Board of Mission and Unity of the Church of England, 1986

35 Prayer of an African Christian in *With All God's People*, World Council of Churches, 1989, quoted by Morley, *Bread of Tomorrow*, p. 27

36 St Augustine, *City of God*, 10.6; Sermons 272, 227, 229

37 Angela Ashwin, *The Book of a Thousand Prayers*, Marshall Pickering, p. 373. Zondervan Edition copyright © 1996, 2002 by Angela Ashwin. Used by permission of The Zondervan Corporation

38 *Worship in an Indian Context*, quoted by Ashwin, *The Book of a Thousand Prayers*

39 Christian Aid – from a leaflet

40 Milner-White, *My God, My Glory*, p. 70

41 Christian Aid – from a leaflet

42 Miller, *Praying the Eucharist*, p. 80

43 Rupert Brooke, 'The great lover', *Rupert Brooke: The Poetical Works*, ed. Geoffrey Keynes, Faber and Faber, 1946, pp. 30–2

44 Elizabeth Jennings, 'I count the moments', *Moments of Grace*, Carcanet, 1979, p. 31

45 W. H. Auden, *Collected Poems*, Faber and Faber, 1976, pp. 447–50

46 Janet Morley, *All Desires Known*, SPCK, 1992

47 Weil, *Waiting on God*, p177

48 Anthony of Sourozh, *Living Prayer*, p. 43

49 No. 17 Czech Litany, *With All God's People*, WCC, 1989, quoted by Morley, *Bread of Tomorrow*

50 Anthony of Sourozh, *Living Prayer*, pp. 32–3

51 J. Neville Ward, *Beyond Tomorrow*, Epworth, 1981, pp. 75–6

52 Kenneth Slack, *Praying the Lord's Prayer Today*, SCM Press, 1973, pp. 112–13

53 From daily worship of 'Your Will be Done – Mission in Christ's Way', San Antonio Conference, 1990 – quoted by Morley, *Bread of Tomorrow*, p. 93

54 Ernest Raymond, *The Bethany Road*, Cassell, 1967, pp. 207–8

55 Miller, *Praying the Eucharist*, p. 95

56 Nicolas Cabasilas, *Life in Christ*, quoted in *Seasons of the Spirit*, selected by George Every, Richard Harries and Kallistos Ware, SPCK, 1984, p. 139

57 From workers in community soup kitchens in the shanty towns of Lima, Peru. Quoted by Morley, *Bread of Tomorrow*, p. 97

58 Morley, *All Desires Known*

59 Irish blessing, *All Year Round*, British Council of Churches, 1987 – quoted by Morley, *Bread of Tomorrow*, p. 189

60 Gregory Dix, *The Shape of the Liturgy*, Dacre, 1945, p. 744